Instant Idea Book
Easy Bulletin Boards
for Elementary Teachers

(includes reproducible pattern pages)

by
Barbara Gruber & Sue Gruber

Illustrations by

Lynn Conklin Power

Copyright© 1987 Frank Schaffer Publications, Inc.
All rights reserved - Printed in the U.S.A.
Published by **Frank Schaffer Publications, Inc.**
1028 Via Mirabel, Palos Verdes Estates, California 90274

ISBN 0-86734-071-1

Table of Contents

Introduction

Easy Bulletin Boards is filled with ideas for attractive, quick-to-do bulletin boards to make your classroom a fun place to learn! Patterns are provided for many bulletin boards and no special materials are required. Student participation is an important part of learning. That's why our bulletin board ideas involve every student. Participation results in a sense of shared responsibility and pride in the classroom. Enjoy creating these special bulletin boards with your students!

Barbara Gruber

Getting Started

Here are hints to help you get the most out of this book!

- Patterns are included for most bulletin boards in this book. Pattern pages can be used in two ways. Copy the pattern page for each student, or use each pattern to make a tagboard pattern for students to trace.

- Wallpaper samples, gift wrap, butcher paper or construction paper may be used to create colorful bulletin boards.
- If the suggested color of paper is not available, students can sponge paint white paper or use a different color.
- Paper tablecloths with holiday themes are perfect for covering classroom bulletin boards. Watch for half-price sales in stationery stores after the holidays.
- Encourage your students to add their own ideas to your bulletin board displays.

Getting Started

- Does your classroom lack bulletin board space? Create a butcher paper banner instead of a bulletin board. Use the banner to brighten a wall, door, or hallway. Consider donating a colorful banner to the school or public library, the school or district office, or the school cafeteria.

- Cut gift wrap into strips to make attractive bulletin board borders. Laminate the strips for extra durability.

- Store bulletin board letters and patterns to use again. Plastic bags or envelopes are ideal for keeping all the bulletin board pieces together. Label the bag or envelope with the page number from *Easy Bulletin Boards* on which that bulletin board is shown. Keep this book and the bags or envelopes together in a box so they are at your finger tips!

FS-8309 Easy Bulletin Boards

Fall Bulletin Boards

Everyone wants a new lunch box for the start of school!

Ideas for Captions:

- All Packed and Ready to Go
- Welcome Back to School!
- A New Lunch Box and a New School Year
- All Set for School

Directions:

1. Cover the bulletin board with paper of any color. Add a caption.
2. Have each student decorate and cut out the lunch box pattern on page 9.
3. Paste lined paper on the back of every lunch box pattern. Students can write about a day at school, their favorite lunch, or draw and label the foods that would make up a nutritious lunch.

Idea! March is National Nutrition Month. Use the lunch box pattern to create an "Eat a Healthy Lunch" bulletin board.

FS-8309 Easy Bulletin Boards

Lunch Box Pattern

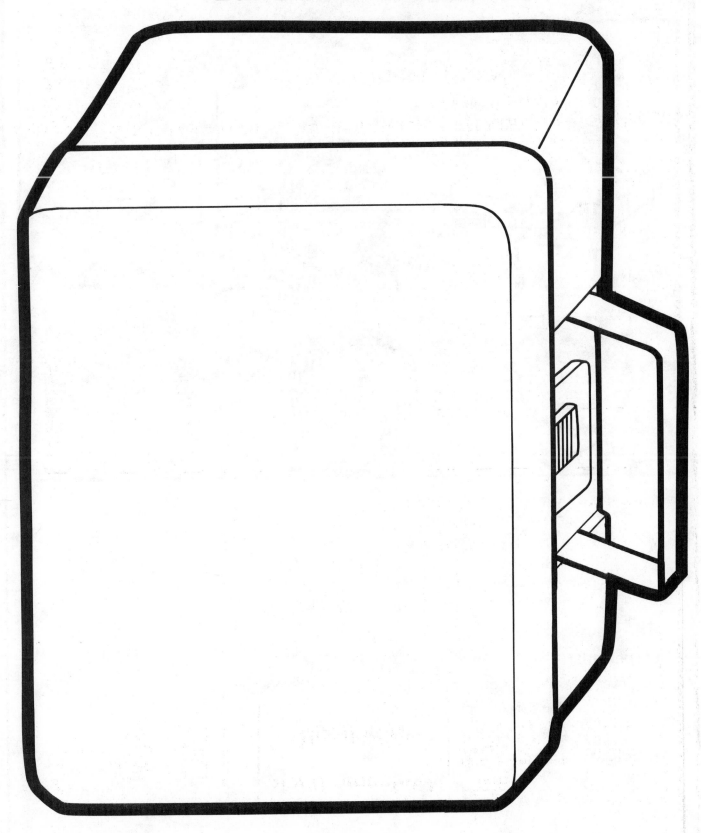

Fall Bulletin Boards

A friendly bulletin board for back-to-school, open house or any time of year!

Ideas for Captions:

- Getting to Know You
- Meet the Gang
- We're Glad to Be Here
- World's Best Class!

Directions:

1. Cover the bulletin board in paper of any color. Add a caption.
2. Reproduce the self-portrait pattern on page 11 for every student.
3. Each child draws a self-portrait in full color and cuts it out.
4. Arrange the self-portraits in rows as shown.

Self-Portrait Pattern

Teacher: Use this self-portrait pattern with page 10.

FS-8309 Easy Bulletin Boards

Fall Bulletin Boards

A bulletin board with colorful leaves brings fall to your classroom.

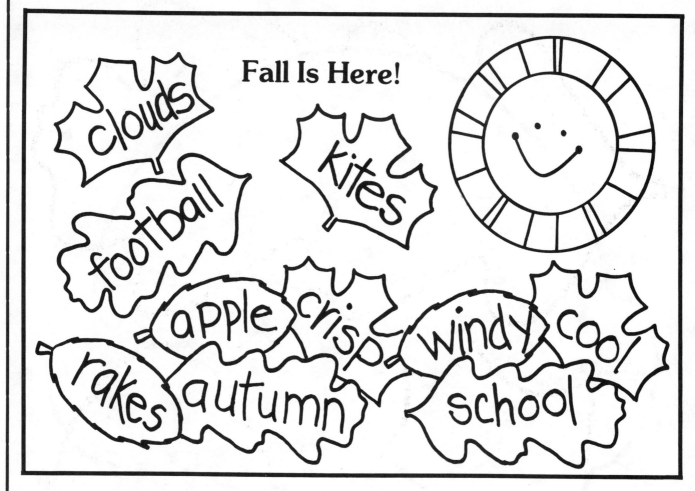

Ideas for Captions:

- Falling Leaves
- The Colors of Autumn
- Fall Is Here!
- The Leaves of Autumn

Directions:

1. Cover the bulletin board with blue paper and add a caption.
2. Have each student cut out and trace the leaf patterns from page 13 on red, gold, light brown, yellow, and orange paper.
3. Then students suggest words that remind them of the fall season. Print each suggestion on a leaf. Pin the leaves on the bulletin board so that they form a pile. Continue adding leaves as new words are suggested by students.

Idea! Leaves can also be used to display reading or spelling vocabulary.

Leaf Patterns

Fall Bulletin Boards

"Grow" a patch of pumpkins to welcome the month of October.

Boo!

David
Sara
Chet
Johnny
Elaine
Lynn
Olga

Ideas for Captions:
- Pumpkin Patrol
- Trick or Treat
- Our Pumpkin Patch
- Welcome Halloween
- Boo!

back

front

yellow paper

Directions:

1. Cover the bulletin board with black paper. Add a yellow moon and pin a few white paper stars across the sky. Cut a landscape from green paper and staple it along the bottom edge of the bulletin board.

2. Have students cut out and trace on orange paper the pumpkin pattern on page 15.

3. Each student draws a face on his pumpkin and adds a green stem, eyes, nose and mouth. Next he cuts out the facial features. Then he glues yellow paper scraps to the back of the pumpkin so the jack-o'-lantern "glows"!

Name _____

Pumpkin Pattern

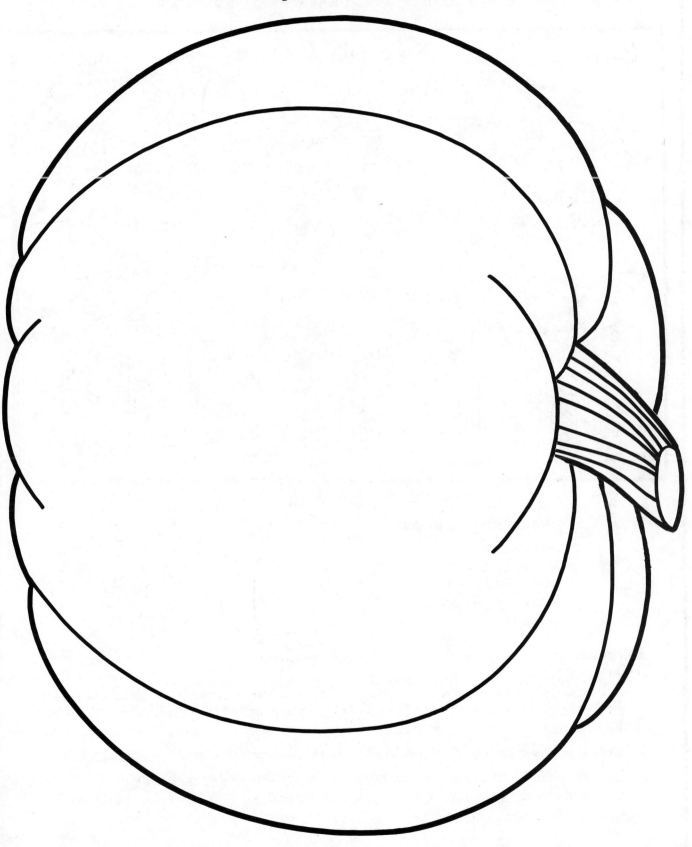

....

Teacher: Use the pumpkin pattern with page 14.

a reproducible page

FS-8309 Easy Bulletin Boards

Winter Bulletin Boards

Add a festive touch to your classroom with an assortment of gift packages.

Especially for You

Ideas for captions:

- Especially for You
- The Perfect Gift
- A Season for Giving
- Holiday Wishes

Directions:

1. Cover the bulletin board in a color of your choice. Add a caption.
2. Have students make colorful gift-wrap designs on the gift box pattern on page 17.
3. Paste lined paper on the back of each gift box. Every student composes a holiday poem or writes about a special gift he would like to give. He can also draw what he imagines inside his box. Then he fills out his gift tag and attaches it with string or yarn to his box.
4. To make the gift boxes extra fancy, add real stick-on bows!

Name _____ Winter

Gift Box Patterns

To _____

From _____

Teacher: Use the gift box and gift tag patterns with page 16.

©Frank Schaffer Publications, Inc.

17

a reproducible page

FS-8309 Easy Bulletin Boards

Winter Bulletin Boards

Brighten a dreary winter day with warm mittens!

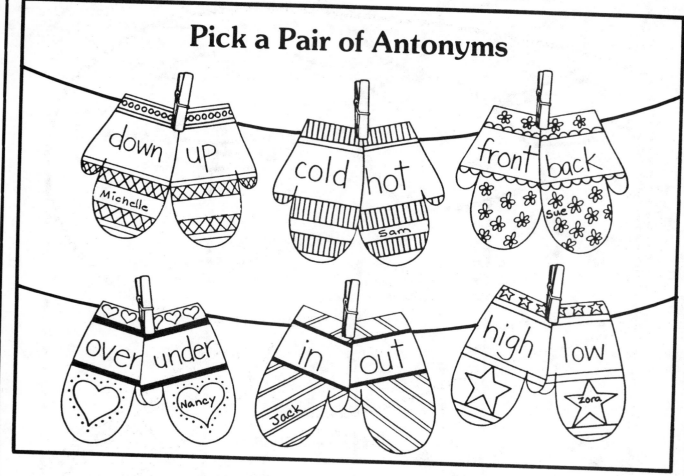

Pick a Pair of Antonyms

down up — Michelle
cold hot — Sam
front back — sue
over under — Nancy
in out — Jack
high low — Zora

Ideas for Captions:
- Brrrr! It's Winter!
- Winter Is Here
- Here Comes Jack Frost!
- Warm Hands and Hearts

Directions:
1. Cover the bulletin board with any color background paper and add a caption.
2. Have each student cut from white paper the pair of mittens and clothespin on page 19. Students decorate their mittens in a design or pattern they like. Remind students to decorate the correct side of each mitten so they have a right and left mitten.
3. Arrange pairs of mittens on the bulletin board. Or, draw rows of clothesline as shown to "hang up" the mittens using the clothespin pattern.
4. Students can also write synonyms, antonyms, or math facts on their pairs of mittens for a "Pick a Pair of..." bulletin board.

Name _____

Mitten and Clothespin Patterns

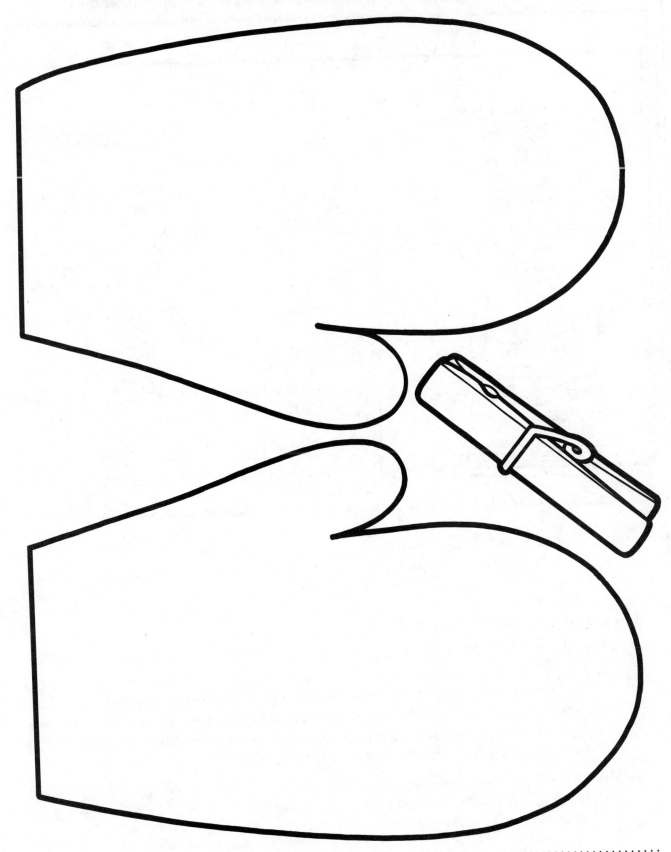

Teacher: Use the mitten and clothespin patterns with page 18.

©Frank Schaffer Publications, Inc.

19

a reproducible page

FS-8309 Easy Bulletin Boards

Winter Bulletin Boards

Presidents and famous Americans are studied in January and February. Students will have fun creating bookmarks to commemorate famous people. After displaying the bookmarks on a bulletin board, they will come in handy in the classroom or school library.

Very Important People

Susan B. Anthony 1820-1906

Walt Disney 1901-1966

A man who developed the animated film into an art form.

Martin Luther King, Jr. 1929-1968

Civil Rights Leader

Ideas for Captions:

- Very Important People!
- Famous Faces
- Introducing Some Famous Americans
- People You Should Know
- Who's Who?

Directions:

1. Cover the bulletin board with paper in a color of your choice. Add a caption.

2. Have students trace the bookmark patterns from page 20 on tagboard or construction paper. Bookmarks should include a portrait of the famous person and dates of that person's life. Information telling why the person is famous can also be included.

Idea! Famous people bookmarks can also be about explorers, authors, inventors, black Americans (February is Black History Month), and women (Womens' History Week is the second week of March beginning on Sunday).

Bookmark Patterns

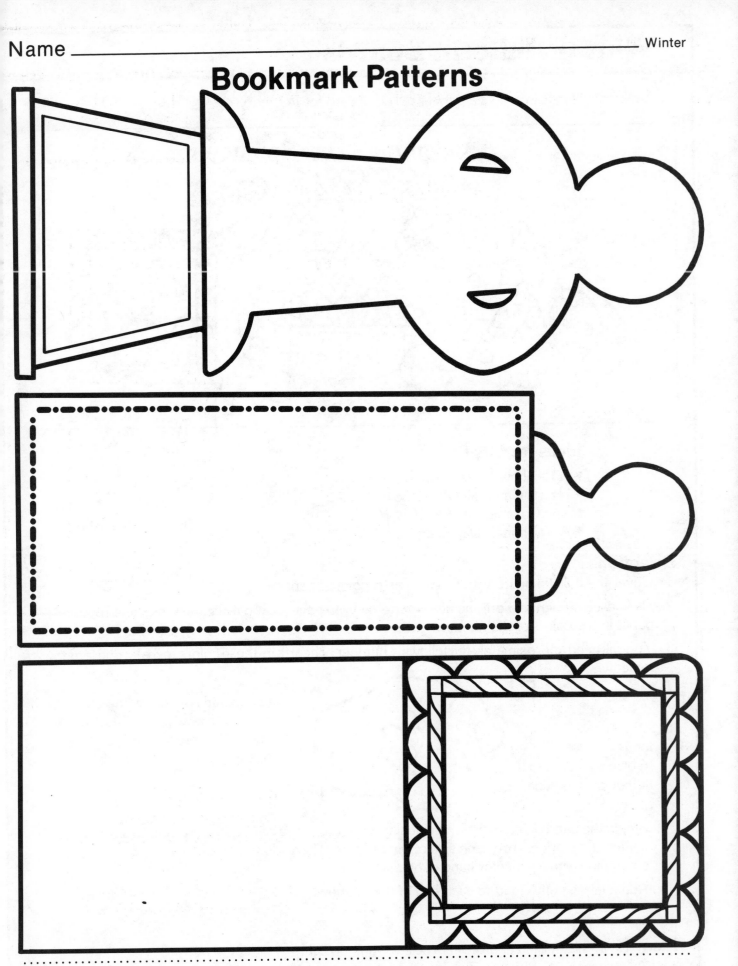

Teacher: Use the bookmark patterns with page 20.

FS-8309 Easy Bulletin Boards

Winter Bulletin Boards

A rainbow of hearts makes a perfect bulletin board for February.

A Valentine's Day Rainbow

Ideas for Captions:

- A Rainbow of Hearts
- Hearts Can Make a Rainbow
- The Colors of the Rainbow
- A Valentine's Day Rainbow

Directions:

1. Cover the bulletin board with blue or pastel-colored paper.

2. Have each student cut out the heart patterns from page 23 and trace them on construction paper in the colors of the rainbow.

3. You will need approximately the following number of hearts in these colors to make one large rainbow.

24 red
22 orange
20 yellow
18 green
16 blue
14 indigo (dark blue)
12 purple

(The bands of colored hearts should be arranged as shown above to represent the colors as they appear in the rainbow.)

4. Staple the band of red hearts individually at the top of the rainbow. It is easier to start at the center and work toward each side of the rainbow. Then add the orange band below the red, continuing with each color band of hearts.

5. Add a large, puffy cloud to each end of the rainbow.

Idea! Tie in this bulletin board with a science unit on light.

Heart Patterns

....

Teacher: Use the heart patterns with page 22.

FS-8309 Easy Bulletin Boards

Spring Bulletin Boards

Kites are fun to fly on a breezy spring day!

Ideas for Captions:

- Flying High
- Caught in the Breeze
- High-Flying Kites
- Go Fly a Kite!

Directions:

1. Cover the bulletin board with blue paper. Add a caption, a yellow sun and a few puffy clouds to the sky.

2. Each student decorates and cuts out the kite patterns on page 25.

3. Give each student a piece of dark-colored yarn approximately twelve inches long. Have students cut out and paste three paper bows on the yarn as shown. Tape the tail to the underside of the kite.

Idea! Lined paper for writing can be pasted on the back of each kite. Students can write a kite poem or a story called "If I Were a Kite."

Kite Patterns

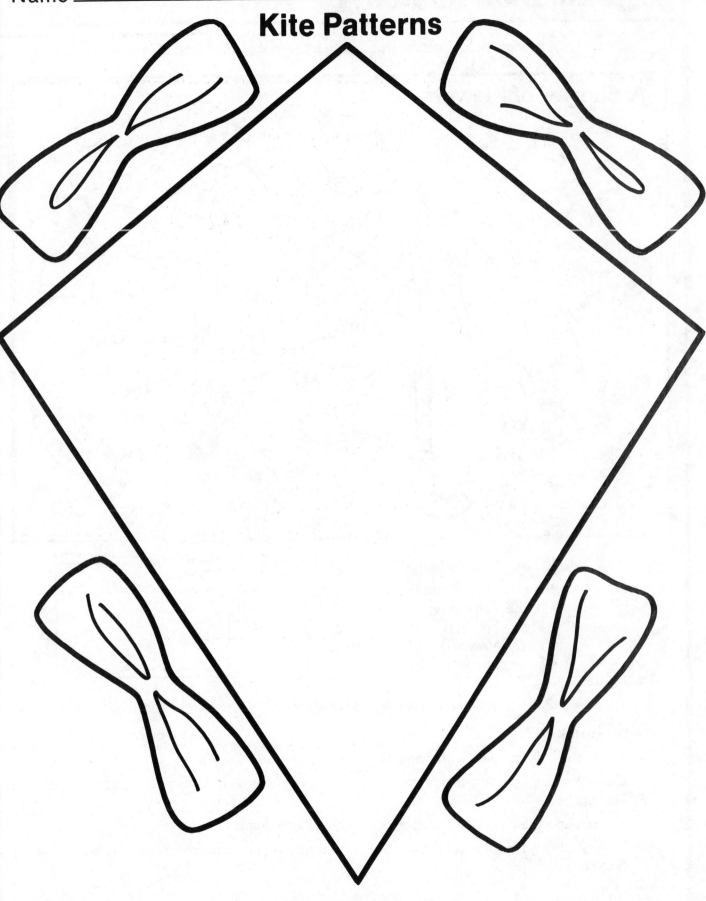

Teacher: Use the kite patterns with page 24.

FS-8309 Easy Bulletin Boards

Spring Bulletin Boards

Add a touch of springtime to your classroom with a colorful combination of umbrellas and flowers!

A Shower of Flowers

Ideas for Captions:
- A Shower of Flowers
- It's Raining Flowers
- Spring Has Sprung
- April Showers Bring May Flowers
- Spring Showers Bring Flowers

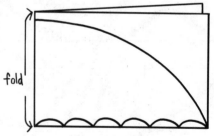

fold

Fold butcher paper. Then sketch and cut out an umbrella.

Directions:

1. Cover the bulletin board with pastel background paper.

2. Cut umbrellas from two different colors of butcher paper. Add umbrella handles cut from black paper.

3. Pin or staple the umbrellas and caption on the bulletin board.

4. Have students decorate, cut out and assemble the flower patterns from page 27 to pin on the bulletin board.

FS-8309 Easy Bulletin Boards

Flower Patterns

Spring Bulletin Boards

A sky full of butterflies will welcome the warm weather!

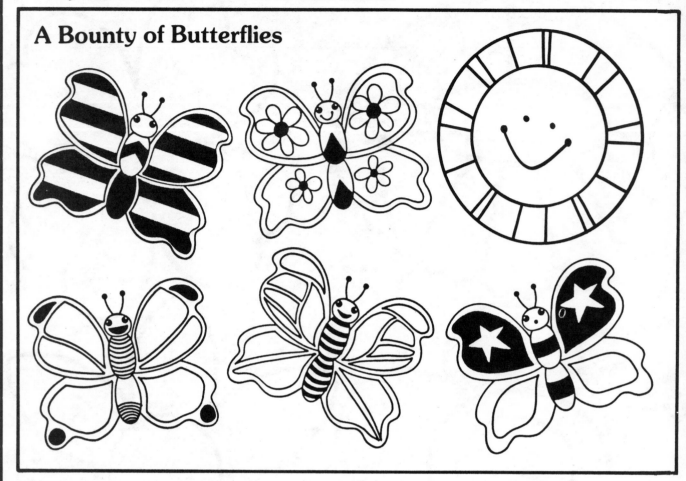

A Bounty of Butterflies

Ideas for Captions:

- A Sky Filled With Butterflies
- Signs of Spring
- Floating and Fluttering
- A Bounty of Butterflies

Directions:

1. Cover the bulletin board with blue paper. Add a caption and a bright yellow sun.
2. Have every student color and cut out the butterfly pattern on page 29.

Idea! Lined paper can be pasted on the back of the butterfly.

Butterfly Pattern

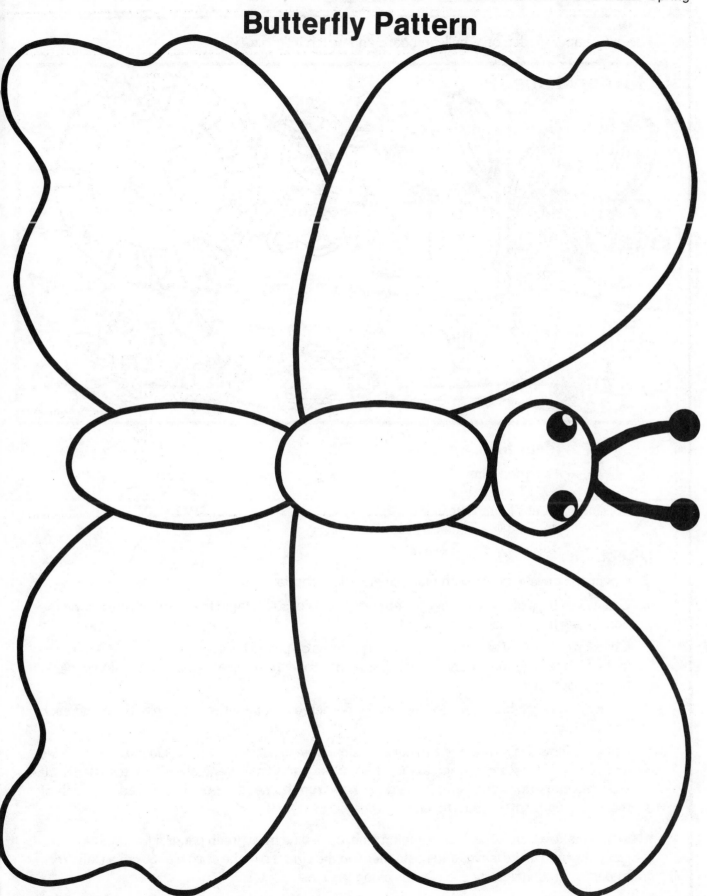

Teacher: Use the butterfly pattern with page 28.

Spring Bulletin Boards

"Plant" a paper garden on a bulletin board and watch it "grow"!

Ideas for Captions:

- Garden Time
- It's Time to Plant!
- Let's Plant Our Garden!
- Spring Is a Time for Growing Things

Directions:

1. Cover the bulletin board with blue paper. Add a caption.
2. Cut wavy strips of brown paper to represent rows of soil. Staple the strips in rows along the bottom section of the bulletin board.
3. Children can cut out and color the garden patterns on page 31. Or, you can use the patterns to make tagboard templates and have the students trace the templates on construction paper in the appropriate colors.
4. "Plant" the vegetables and seedlings in the garden by slipping the paper plants behind each row of strips.
5. Have students design and add a paper sun, clouds, seed packets, worms, ladybugs, butterflies and grasshoppers. Encourage students to make additional "vegetables" for the garden. If students can bring actual empty seed packets from home, the pouches will add a touch of realism to your garden bulletin board.

Idea! To make a leafy squash or pumpkin vine, cut a vine from green paper. Have students use the leaf pattern to make leaves and paste them on the vine. To make corn plants, cut a stalk from green paper. Students paste corn leaves along the stalk.

Garden Patterns

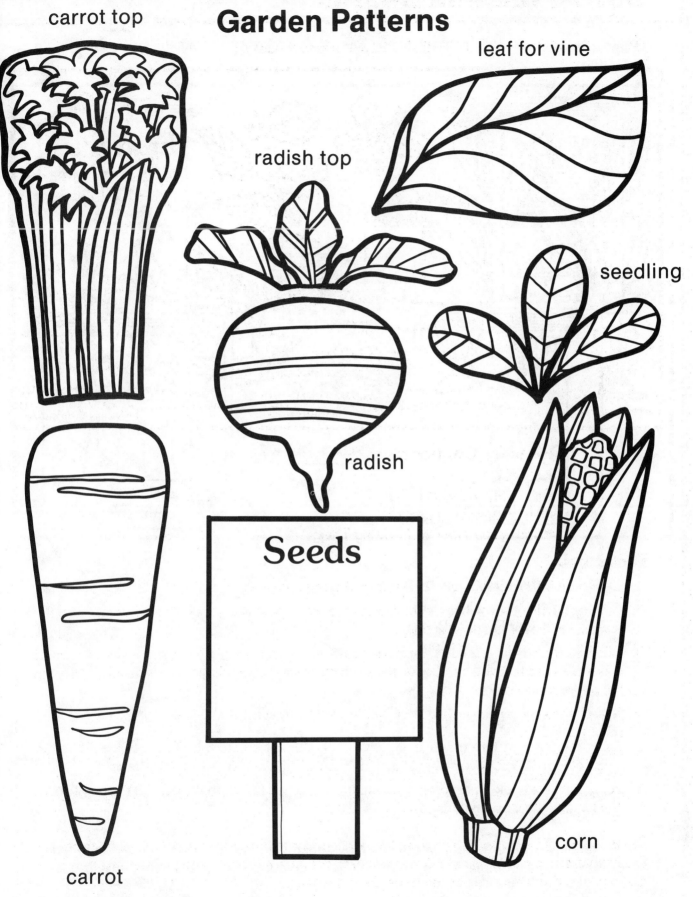

carrot top

leaf for vine

radish top

seedling

radish

Seeds

corn

carrot

Bulletin Boards for Any Time of Year

Create a high-interest bulletin board about your students' favorite books. Include your favorite book, too!

Ideas for Captions:
- We Love To Read!
- Our Favorite Books!
- My Favorite Story
- Look at a Book

Directions:
1. Cover the bulletin board with paper of any color.
2. Using the book pattern on page 33, have each student create a book cover for his or her favorite book. Book covers should include the title, the author and an illustration.
3. To make this a book report project, students paste lined paper on the back of the book cover and write a summary of the story.

Idea! National Children's Book Week is in November. National Library Week is celebrated in April. Your class can commemorate these special weeks with a "We Love to Read" bulletin board.

Book Pattern

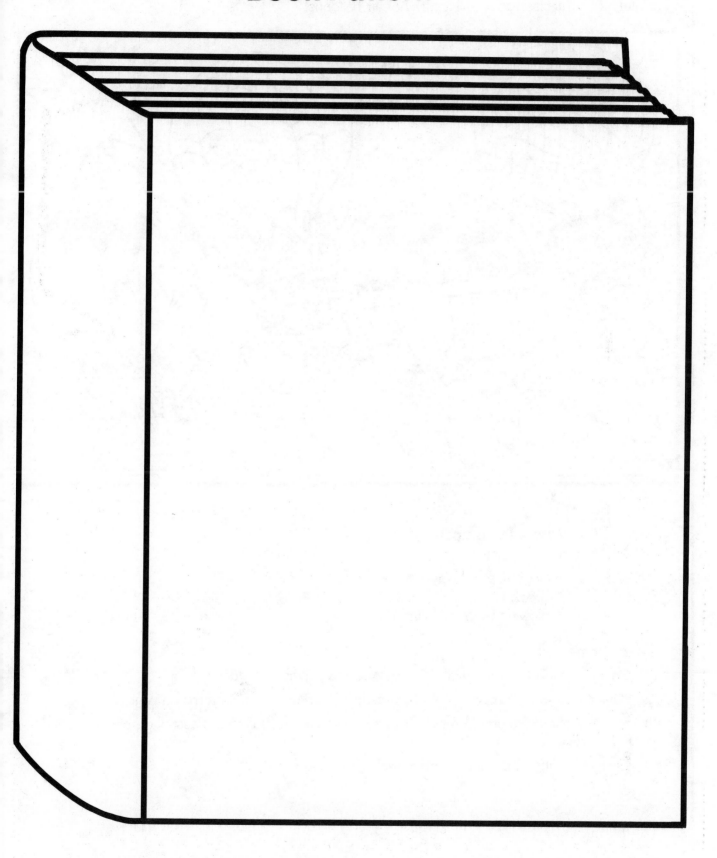

Bulletin Boards for Any Time of Year

Make a colorful classroom—fill it with hot-air balloons!

Ideas for Captions:

- Flying High
- Up, Up, and Away
- Breezing By
- Blowing With the Wind

Directions:

1. Cover the bulletin board with blue background paper and add a caption.
2. Have every student make a colorful hot-air balloon using the patterns on page 35.
3. Students should color and cut out the passengers for the balloons. Passengers can be pasted in the basket.
4. Then add puffy white clouds and a bright yellow sun!

Hot-Air Balloon Patterns

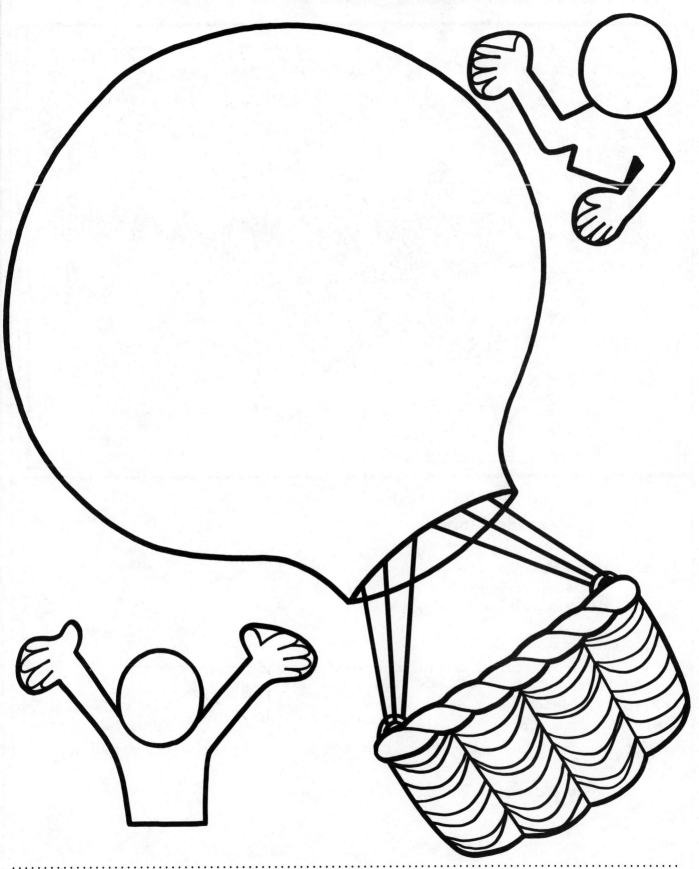

Bulletin Boards for Any Time of Year

Everyone loves ice cream! Let each student create her favorite ice cream cone.

We All Scream for Ice Cream!

Ideas for Captions:

- We All Scream for Ice Cream!
- Yum, Yum
- A Cool Treat
- A Treat to Eat

Directions:

1. Cover the bulletin board with paper of any color. Add a caption.
2. Have students cut out and trace the ice cream cone patterns on page 37 to make their own cone and scoops of ice cream. The paper scoops of ice cream can be pasted on the cone.
3. Students can decorate their ice cream by drawing bright red cherries, chocolate sprinkles, or nuts.
4. Have every student print her name on her ice cream cone.

Ice Cream Cone Patterns

Bulletin Boards for Any Time of Year

Lovable teddy bears make a great addition to any classroom.

Teddy Bear Friends

Ideas for Captions:
- Teddy Bear Hall of Fame
- Teddy Bear Friends
- Everyone Loves Teddy Bears
- Teddy Bears Go to School

Directions:
1. Cover the bulletin board with paper of any color. Add a caption.
2. Have each student make a teddy bear using the patterns on pages 39 to 41.
3. Students cut out then trace the clothing patterns on colored paper. Clothing can be decorated with buttons, belts, stripes and other details. Use these patterns to make jogging suits, pajamas or other outfits. The clothes can be pasted on the bears.
4. Students can add additional objects to the bears such as jewelry, glasses or wristwatches.

©Frank Schaffer Publications, Inc.   FS-8309 Easy Bulletin Boards

Teddy Bear Pattern

Teddy Bear Clothing Patterns

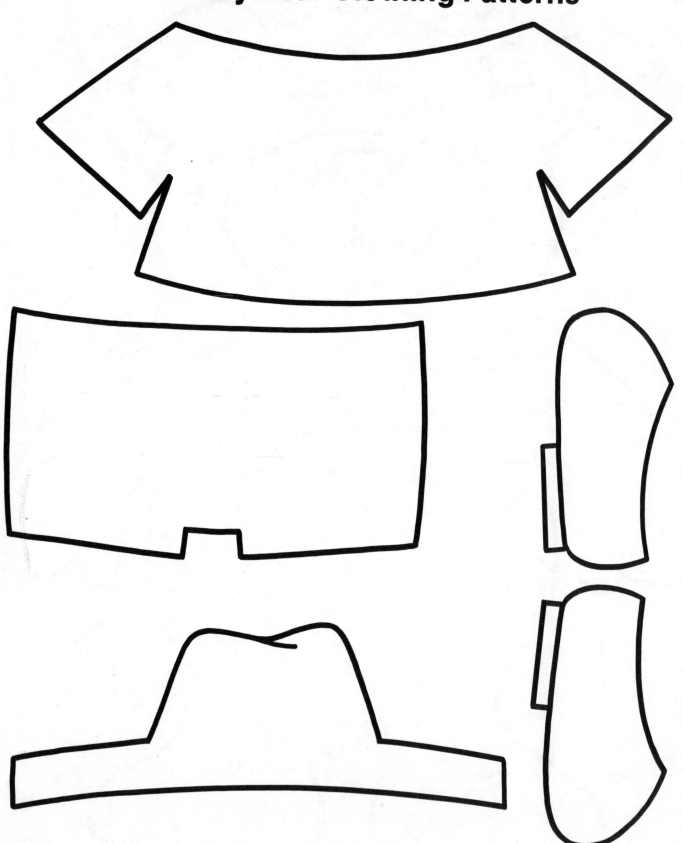

Teacher: Use the clothing patterns with pages 38 and 39.

©Frank Schaffer Publications, Inc.

40
a reproducible page

FS-8309 Easy Bulletin Boards

Teddy Bear Clothing Patterns

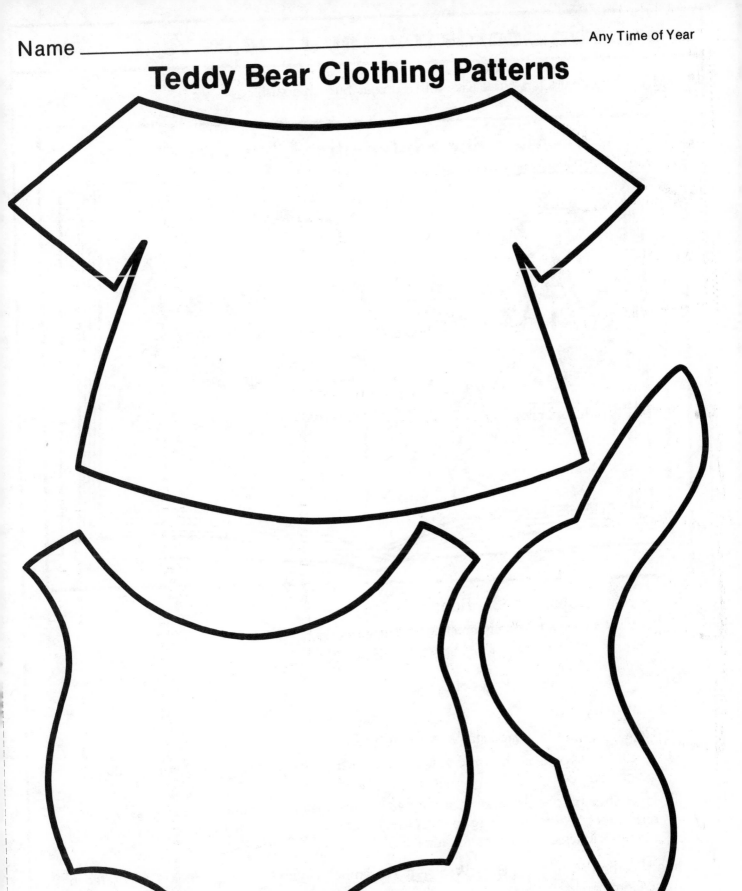

Teacher: Use the clothing patterns with pages 38, 39 and 40.

FS-8309 Easy Bulletin Boards

Bulletin Boards for Any Time of Year

Make book characters come alive with a unique bulletin board.

Ideas for Captions:
- Meet Some Interesting Characters
- Our Favorite Characters
- Storybook People
- From the Pages of Books

Directions:

1. Cover the bulletin board with paper of any color.
2. Cut a large book, as shown above, from butcher paper. Staple or pin it in the center of a bulletin board.
3. Have students use the patterns on page 43 to make their favorite book characters. Post these character cut-outs on the large book. On each label print the character's name and the title of the book in which the character appears.

Idea! National Children's Book Week is in November. National Library Week is celebrated in April. Commemorate these special weeks with a bulletin board filled with book characters.

Name _____ Any Time of Year

Book Character Patterns

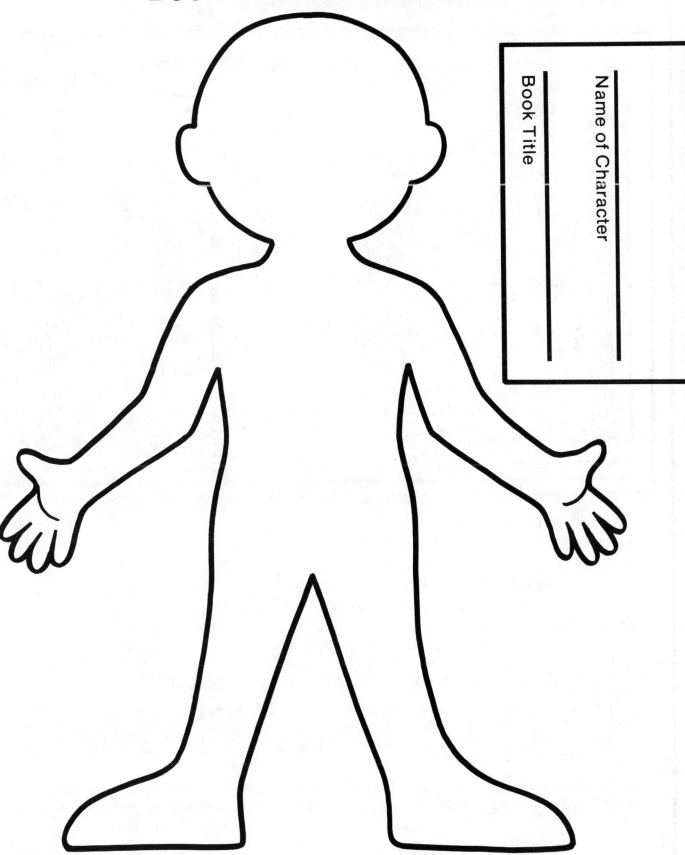

Name of Character _____

Book Title _____

Bulletin Boards for Any Time of Year

Line up a parade of trucks for a colorful bulletin board display.

Ideas for Captions:

- Trucking Along
- Convoy Coming Through
- Beep! Beep!
- Rolling Along

Directions:

1. Cover the bulletin board with brightly colored paper and add a caption.
2. Each student uses the truck pattern on page 45 to make a truck for the bulletin board. Tell students to decorate their truck according to its use. If it is a moving van, it would have the name of a moving company on its side. If it is a truck making deliveries to a market, decorate it with foods or other goods.
3. Tell students to be sure to draw a person driving the truck.
4. Staple the completed trucks in rows.

Truck Pattern

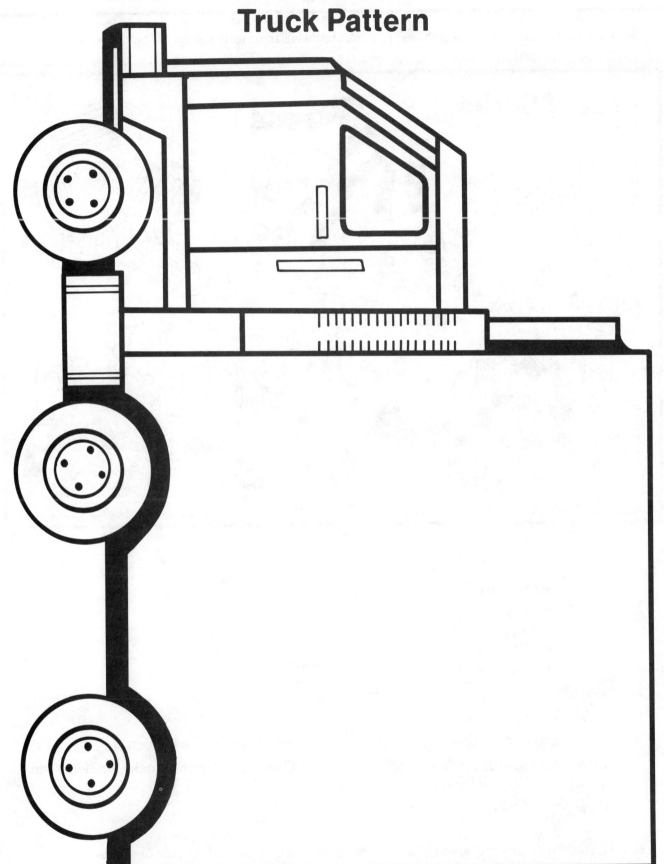

Bulletin Boards for Any Time of Year

Socks come in many colors and styles. Your students will have fun designing a pair of socks for the class bulletin board!

Ideas for Captions:

- Sock It to Me
- Crazy Socks
- Pick a Pair
- Lots of Socks!

Directions:

1. Cover the bulletin board with paper in a color of your choice. Add a caption.
2. Have each student use the sock patterns on page 47 to design a pair of socks. Students can add lace and decorations to their socks.
3. Pin the pairs of socks on the board.

Idea! Students can write synonyms, antonyms, or math facts on their pair of socks.

Sock Patterns

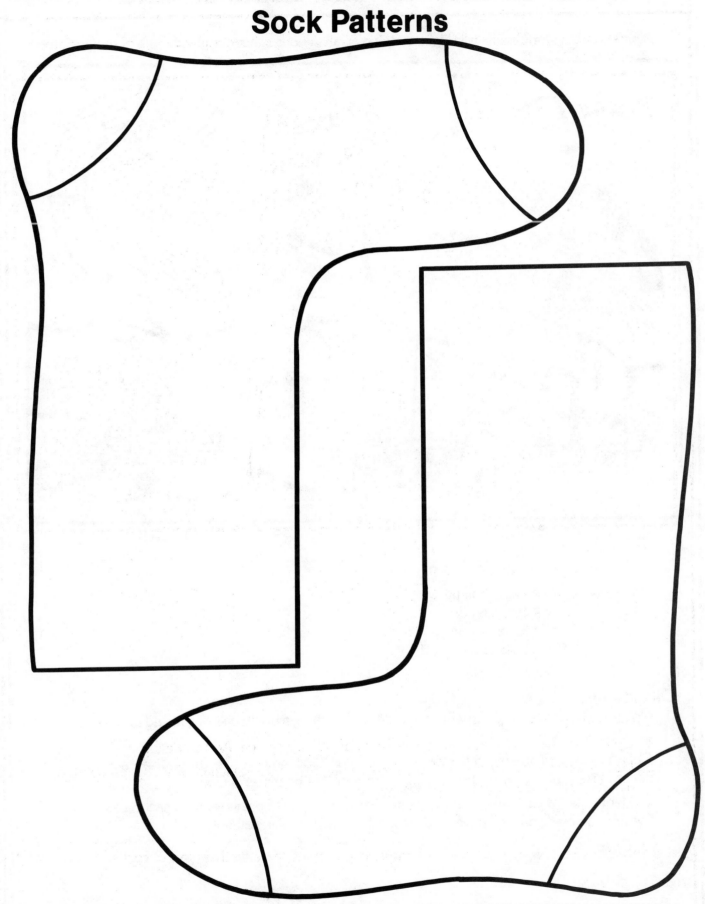

Bulletin Boards for Any Time of Year

Sailboats with colorful sails will brighten up any wall in your classroom.

Sailing Along

Ideas for Captions:

- Sailing Along
- Breezing By
- Ships Ahoy!
- Sails in the Wind

Directions:

1. Cover the bulletin board with white paper. Add a caption, a bright yellow sun and a few birds in the sky.

2. Cut wavy strips of blue paper to represent waves in the ocean or a lake. Staple the strips of blue paper in rows along the bottom section of the bulletin board as shown.

3. Students use the sailboat pattern on page 49 to design colorful sails for their sailboats. Before "setting the boats afloat," have students add a sailor to their sailboat.

Sailboat Pattern

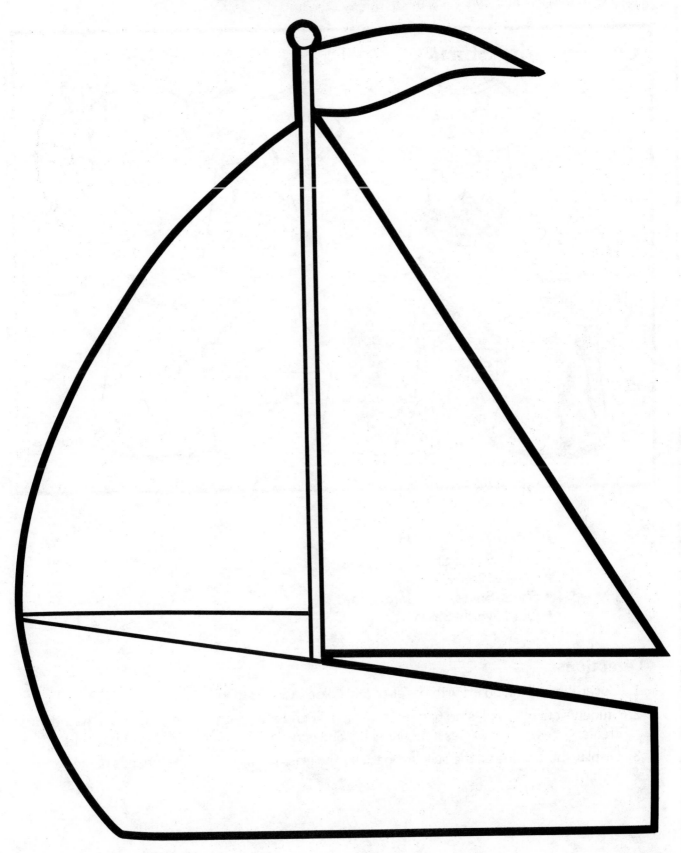

FS-8309 Easy Bulletin Boards

Bulletin Boards for Any Time of Year

It's fun to design your own T-shirt!

Our Favorite Shirts

(Frogs are No. 1 — Kelly; Jean; STATE U — Kemal; Eric; APPLE — Phyllis; Laura)

Ideas for Captions:

- Look at That Shirt!
- Original T-Shirts
- Shirts, Shirts, and More Shirts
- Our Favorite Shirts

Directions:

1. Cover the bulletin board with paper of any color. Add a caption.
2. Students cut out the T-shirt pattern from page 51 and trace it on colored paper. Each student creates a design and pastes it on her shirt. She can also decorate the back of her shirt.
3. Display the T-shirts on the bulletin board for the class to enjoy. Pin the student's name by her T-shirt.

T-Shirt Pattern

Bulletin Boards for Any Time of Year

This bulletin board provides a place for students to share their thoughts on a variety of subjects!

Ideas for Captions:

- People Are Talking
- What's on Your Mind?
- If I Had Three Wishes
- My Hero Is...Because...
- My Hobby Is...

Directions:

1. Cover the bulletin board with paper of any color. Add a caption.

2. Each student uses the pattern on page 53 to make a "talk bubble." Lined writing paper can be pasted on the bubbles. Arrange the cut-out conversation bubbles on a bulletin board.

3. If students wish to make a "think bubble" instead of a talk bubble, they can change the shape of the bubble as shown below.

think bubble

©Frank Schaffer Publications, Inc.

FS-8309 Easy Bulletin Boards

Name _____

"Talk Bubble" Pattern

··

Teacher: Use the bubble pattern with page 52.

FS-8309 Easy Bulletin Boards

Bulletin Boards for Any Time of Year

Everyone enjoys receiving an award! This bulletin board makes everyone feel special!

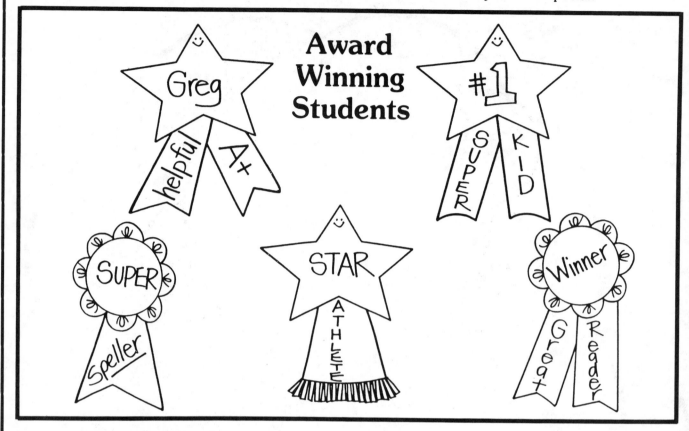

Ideas for Captions:
- We're Terrific!
- Award Winning Students
- We're the Champions!
- I'm Glad to Be Me!

Directions:

1. Cover the bulletin board with paper of any color. Add a caption.

2. Have students design awards using the award patterns on page 55. Students cut construction paper ribbons to attach to their awards.

Ideas!

- Each student selects something she likes about herself. Then the student designs an award honoring her achievement.

- Place students' names in an envelope. Every student draws a name and creates an award for that person.

- Every student creates an award for his favorite book or television show to pin on a bulletin board titled "We Salute the Best!"

- Students make awards for people who have helped them.

- Students select their best work for the day or week. Each person designs an award to attach to his work.

Award Patterns

Bulletin Boards for Any Time of Year

A bunch of balloons fly high on this bulletin board!

Hold on Tightly!

Deo   Claude   Derek   Megan   Rowena

Ideas for Captions:
- A Bunch of Balloons
- Hold on Tightly!
- Balloons for Everyone
- We Love Balloons!

Directions:
1. Cover the bulletin board with paper of any color. Add a caption.
2. Have each student cut out and trace a handprint from the patterns on page 64. Students use white, tan, or pink paper. Next they outline their handprint with black crayon and print their name on it as shown.
3. Then each student cuts out the balloon pattern on page 57 and traces it onto colored paper. Students decorate their balloon with designs, pictures or messages.
4. Staple the handprints at the bottom of the bulletin board as shown. Then staple each child's balloon on the bulletin board and draw a string to his or her handprint.

Balloon Pattern

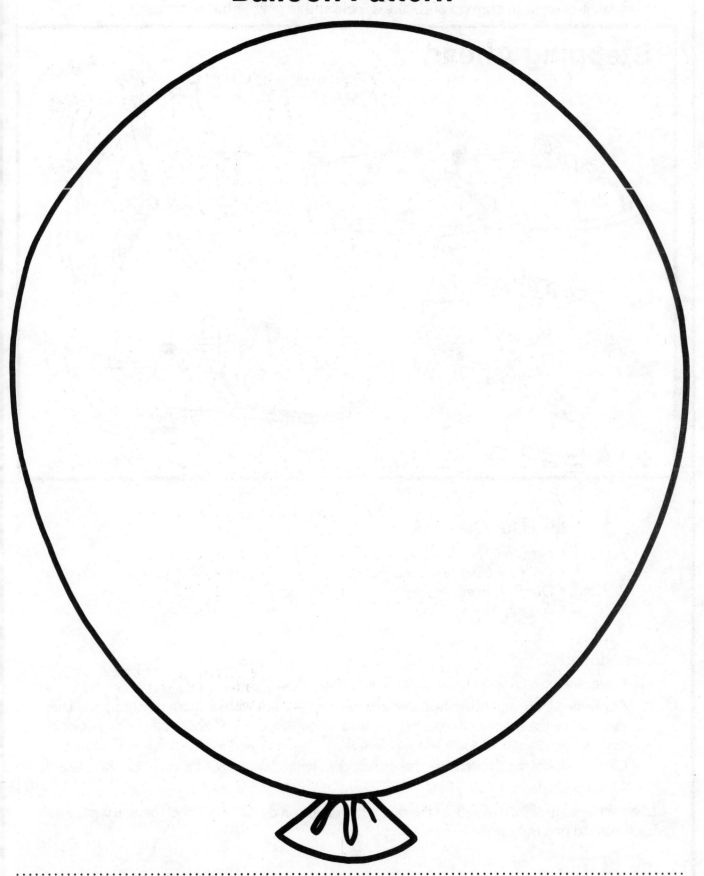

Teacher: Use the balloon pattern with page 56.

Bulletin Boards for Any Time of Year

Everyone will want to step up and take a look at this unique bulletin board!

Stepping Ahead

Ideas for Captions:

- Stepping Ahead
- On Your Mark, Get Set, Go!
- Our Best Feet Forward
- Jogging Along

Directions:

1. Cover the bulletin board with paper of any color. Add a caption.
2. Students cut out and trace the shoe pattern on page 59 twice to make a pair of shoes. They can change the shape of the shoe to create a pair of "high tops." Shoes can be any color or design. Fancy shoelaces can be added, too!
3. On the back of the shoe shapes, have each child write a story about someplace she'd like to go.

Ideas! Have students write about the things their feet can do. Or, have each person write what his shoes did one night while he was asleep!

Shoe Pattern

Banners

Brighten a hall, wall or door with a colorful, quick-to-create banner! Use a strip of butcher paper that is five or six feet long.

Green Tree Banner
Cut green cloud shapes and a brown tree trunk. Paste on a banner to form a tree.

Back-to-School Banner
Using the apple pattern on page 61, make an apple for every child in your class to pin on a back-to-school banner. Print each child's name on his or her apple. Add the perfect caption, "You Are the Apple of My Eye!"

Fall-Is-Here Banner
Students use the patterns on page 61 to make a "Fall Is Here!" banner with squirrels and acorns in the tree.

A Springtime Banner
To create a "Welcome Spring" banner, students use the patterns on page 62. They make birds and bird nests for a colorful display.

Love a Tree for Arbor Day

Idea! Celebrate International Arbor Day in December by making a tree banner. Honor National Wildlife Week (the third week of March) with a spring banner.

Fall Patterns

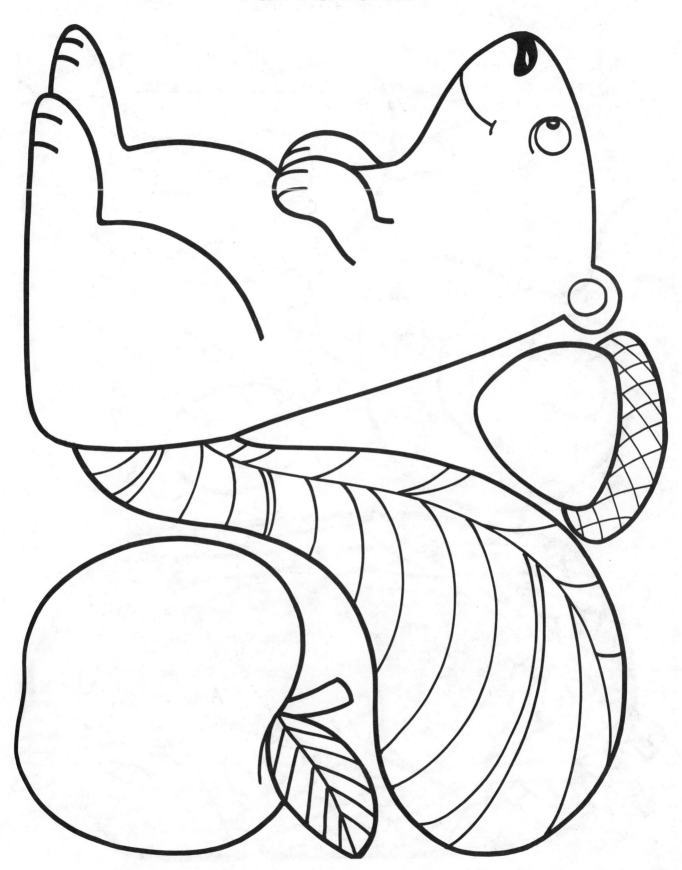

Spring Patterns

Teacher: Use the spring patterns with page 60.

a reproducible page

Banners

Handprint Banners!

Use the handprint patterns on page 64, or have students help each other trace outlines of their hands on a variety of brightly colored paper.

Hello Banner

Paste the handprints on a butcher paper banner with the caption, Our Class Says Hello. Use this as a welcome banner for open house by printing each child's name on his or her handprint.

All-About-Me Handprints!

Each student draws his face on the palm of the paper handprint. Students write about themselves on each finger as shown.

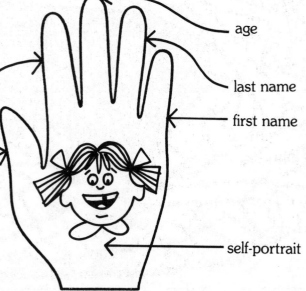

Handprint Patterns

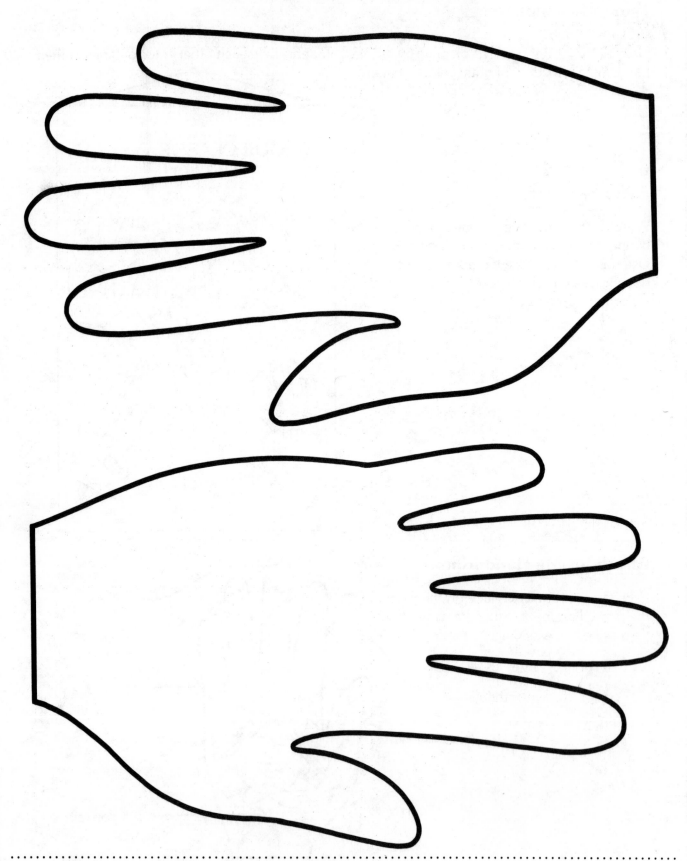

Teacher: Use the handprint patterns with pages 56 and 63.

FS-8309 Easy Bulletin Boards